Introducing

1 Peter

Charles Ozanne

ISBN: 978-1-78364-510-7

www.obt.org.uk

Quotations are from the *Revised Standard Version*
unless otherwise stated.

****

The Open Bible Trust
Fordland Mount, Upper Basildon,
Reading, RG8 8LU, UK.

Introducing 1 Peter

Contents

Introduction

Introduction

This book is not a commentary on 1 Peter, but simply an introduction. I have tried to answer such questions as to whom it was written and where from, and to give a brief survey of its character and contents. There are already many useful conmmentaries in existence, both short ones by A.M. Stibbs (1959) and C.E.B. Cranfield (1961), and longer ones by E.G. Selwyn (1946) and J.N.D. Kelly (1969) - to mention only a few. This booklet will meet head on, and hopefully answer convincingly, a few questions concerning which the commentators are notoriously unreliable, questions of particular relevance to dispensational truth.

After a brief discussion on the authorship of the epistle, I have made a comparison of Peter's theology and Paul's. Reasons are given for believing those doctrines and ideas which we associate with Paul are not to be found in Peter's first epistle (or indeed any other New Testament writings). The next section deals with the vexed question as to what class of person is addressed in this epistle. It shows that the first recipients of this letter were Jews and proselytes (as on the day of Pentecost). Arguments to the contrary are shown to have no sure foundation.

Having settled that point, I have gone on to discuss points of Jewish interest. A number of passages are adduced which are far more appropriate if addressed to Jews rather than Gentiles. In the last section I have focused on some of Peter's recurring themes, such as Rebirth, Hope, Rejoicing and Suffering, all of which are as relevant to us Gentiles today as to the Christian Jews to whom the letter was originally sent.

Last but not least, I have discussed in the Appendix the geographical provenance of this epistle and of Peter's ministry at that time. Of the two rival opinions, Babylon and Rome, the reasons are given for preferring Babylon. Not least of these is that Peter clearly states that he wrote from Babylon!

The Author of
1 Peter

The Author of 1 Peter

There should be no question concerning the author of this epistle seeing that it begins with the words "Peter, an apostle of Jesus Christ ..." Most commentators are in fact prepared to admit that the apostle Peter was in some way involved in the writing of this epistle. The chief objection to ascribing it wholly to him is the quality of the Greek. Stylistically the Greek of 1 Peter is some of the best in the New Testament and doubt has been expressed whether Peter, who is described as "unlettered" or "unschooled" (Acts 4:13, *NIV*), would have been equal to the task.

The solution has been found in the part played by Silvanus. Peter says, "By (by means of) Silvanus, a faithful brother as I regard him, I have written briefly to you" (5:12). The verb "written" suggests something more than simply writing it out at Peter's dictation. Probably Silvanus was responsible for drafting the letter on Peter's behalf and on his instructions. Writes J.N.D. Kelly:

> "It seems reasonable to attribute to him (Silvanus) the refinement of Greek grammar and style and the literary vocabulary, while at the same time recognising in the letter the message, the apostolic authority and, to some extent at any rate, the personality of Peter."

It is generally agreed that this Silvanus is to be identified with Silas who was a companion and "fellow preacher" with Paul (2 Corinthians 1:19; 1 Thessalonians 1:1; 2 Thessalonians 1:1). Silas (*NIV*; Silvanus, *RSV*) had been joint author with Paul of two epistles and here, assuming the same person is meant, we find him joint author with Peter of another epistle. If this is a true assessment, it would seem to indicate a healthy cross-fertilization between the ministries of Peter and Paul.

Peter
and Paul

Peter and Paul

In the section after this we will have a closer look at 1 Peter to find out what precisely it does say. In this section I am more interested in what it does *not* say, though at the same time we shall discover a few things that it does say as well. Some people have considered 1 Peter the most Pauline epistle in the New Testament outside of Paul's own writings. But in point of fact the doctrines and ideas we associate with Paul are almost completely absent from 1 Peter. J.N.D. Kelly has this to say:

> "... his theology is in important respects different from, and markedly less advanced than, the Apostle's. He has no inkling, for example, of justification by faith, of the tension between faith and works, of the problem of the Law, or of the Church as the body of Christ; indeed, the terms 'church' (62 times in Paul), and 'cross' and 'crucify' (18 times), are totally lacking. His own caste of mind is Hebraic, and this comes out, e.g., in his definitely OT doctrine of God, to Whom he restricts the title 'Lord', and in his conception of the relation of Christians to Israel." (p.15)

He goes on to point out that "sin" for Peter is the concrete act as opposed to the sin-principle in fallen man; that "flesh" is neutral for Peter, not the seat of the sinful nature; and that his view of Christ's sufferings as providing an example to be followed is not a Pauline theme. To these we could add that Paul's doctrine of identification with Christ in His death and resurrection is unknown to Peter.

The fact is that to Paul was given "the gospel of the uncircumcision", a specific body of truth which he received by revelation from Jesus Christ (Galatians 1:11,12). This doctrine was so exclusively his that he refers to it as "my gospel" (Romans 2:16; 16:25; 2 Timothy 2:8). Its terms are not to be found in 1 Peter or any other New Testament writing. On the other hand, Peter was certainly familiar with some of Paul's epistles. He says as much in 2 Peter 3:15,16. It is not surprising therefore if there are a few turns of phrase which he may have borrowed from Paul. The most likely of these is the peculiarly Pauline expression "in Christ" (some 164 times), which is also found three times in 1 Peter (3:16; 5:10,14).

The first sentence we shall look at is one which Peter has in common with two of Paul's epistles.

1 Peter 1:3: "Blessed be the God and Father of our Lord Jesus Christ! By his great mercy we have been born anew (regenerated) to a living hope through the resurrection of Jesus Christ from the dead."

With this compare:

> 2 Corinthians 1:3,4 - "Blessed be the God and Father of our Lord Jesus Christ, the Father of mercies and God of all comfort, who comforts us in all our affliction..."

> Ephesians 1:3 - "Blessed be the God and Father of our Lord Jesus Christ, who has blessed us in Christ with every spiritual blessing in the heavenly places."

It is possible that Peter borrowed these words from 2 Corinthians, or they may have been in regular use among Christians at that time. Especially interesting are the clauses which follow. In 1 Peter, as elsewhere in this epistle, it is a living hope awaiting them in the future. In Ephesians, however, it is the blessing already received in the heavenly places in Christ.

Some people make much of the supposed likeness of 1 Peter to Ephesians. In fact the only other parallel of more than two words is the piece of advice (much needed, I'm sure), "Wives, be subject to your husbands"! (1 Pet.3:1; Ephesians 5:22).

1 Peter 2:11: "Beloved, I beseech you as aliens and exiles to abstain from the passions of the flesh that wage war against your soul."

It is most unlikely that Paul's doctrine of the flesh is reflected here. Elsewhere *sarx* ("flesh") is a morally neutral term in 1 Peter (see 1:24; 3:18,21; 4:1,2,6). What are here called "passions of the flesh", in 1 Peter 4:2 are "passions of men" or "human passions".

Likewise *psuche*, soul, describes "the man himself, considered as a living being or person" (Kelly). There is no suggestion that flesh and soul are distinct parts of human nature. See also 1 Peter 1:9 ("the salvation of your souls"); 1:22 ("having purified your souls"); 2:25 ("the Shepherd and Guardian of your souls"); 3:20 ("eight souls were saved by water"); 4:19 ("entrust their souls to a faithful Creator"). This is also the meaning in Paul's epistles, and throughout the Bible.

1 Peter 2:19,20: "For one is approved (lit. "for this is grace") if, mindful of God, he endures pain while suffering unjustly. For what credit is it, if when you do wrong and are beaten for it you take it patiently? But if when you do right and suffer for it you take it patiently, you have God's approval (lit. "this is favour with God")."

The word *charis*, grace or favour, here means "an act which is intrinsically attractive, and thus wins God's approval." Kelly notes how unlike this is to Paul's use of "grace". Peter uses the word in the same sense as in Luke 6:32-4 where it is translated "What *credit* is that to you?"

The other occurrences of *charis* in 1 Peter include 1:2 ("May grace and peace be multiplied to you"); 1:10,13 (of the salvation which would come their way at the revelation of Jesus Christ); 3:7 (of the gracious gift of life); 4:10 (of God's varied bounty); 5:5 (of the good things bestowed on the humble, in the words of Proverbs 3:34); 5:10,12 (of the God of all help and favour).

1 Peter 2:24: "He himself bore our sins in his body on the tree, that we might die to sin and live to righteousness. By his wounds you have been healed."

Peter's words are reminiscent of Romans 6 where Paul teaches the believer's identification with Christ in His death on the cross. Compare Romans 6:11, "So you also must consider (reckon) yourselves dead to sin and alive to God in Christ Jesus." And 6:13, "yield yourselves to God as men who have been brought from death to life, and your members to God as instruments of righteousness."

However, Kelly translates, "... so that, having broken with our sins, we might live for righteousness." The verb *apoginomai*, while it can mean to die, in its original and natural meaning is "to be away from, have no part in, cease from."

It is doubtful whether Paul's doctrine is really taught here. According to Kelly, "the distinctively Pauline theology of a mystical union and death with Christ in baptism is only obscurely discernible." Selwyn is emphatic that "the mysticism of Rom.6 is conspicuously absent from St. Peter's teaching."

> "The similarity of construction (he says) must not lead us to impute to St. Peter here the mystical doctrine found in Romans 6; his thought is ethical and psychological rather than mystical, and the phrase is best translated 'having ceased from' or 'having abandoned'."

Rather similar is the thought in 1 Peter 4:1,2, "Since therefore Christ suffered in the flesh, arm yourselves with the same thought, for whoever has suffered in the flesh has ceased from sin, so as to live for the rest of the time in the flesh no longer by human passions but by the will of God."

The thought seems to be that suffering has the salutary effect of making one cease from a life devoted to sin, so as to live the rest of one's life by the will of God. In both passages a clean break is implied between the sins of one's former life and the life of righteousness lived thereafter to the will of God. This is achieved, not only by Christ's vicarious suffering (2:24), but also by their own suffering after Christ's example (4:1). Paul's doctrine of *reckoning* is far from Peter's thought.

The elect sojourners of the Dispersion

The elect sojourners of the Dispersion

Peter's First Epistle is addressed to "the elect sojourners of the Dispersion of Pontus, Galatia, Cappadocia, Asia, and Bithynia" (*RV*). The three opening words of this address *eklektoi* (elect), *parepidemoi* (sojourners), and *diaspora* (dispersion) all have strong Jewish associations.

Israel prided itself on its elect status, the fact that God had chosen them out of all the nations of the world. See Deuteronomy 4:37; 7:6; 14:2; Psalm 105:6; Isaiah 45:4; Romans 9:11; 1 Peter 2:9. In the New Testament of course the word is used more commonly of Christians in general, regardless of race or social status.

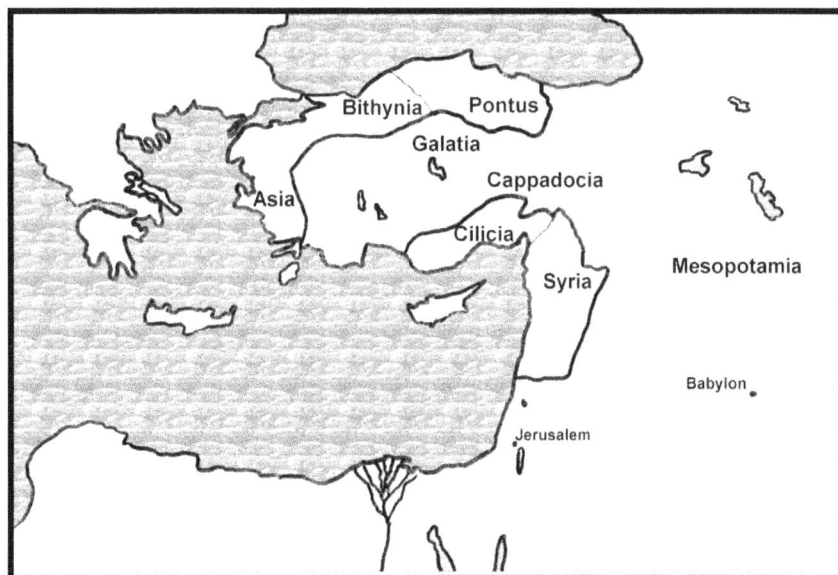

Parepidemos, sojourner, is "a term which connotes one who is merely passing through a territory, with no intention of permanent residence" (J.N.D. Kelly). In the New Testament it occurs twice again - 1 Peter 2:11 ("Beloved, I beseech you as aliens and exiles", *paroikiois kai parepidemois*) and Hebrews 11:13 ("These all died in faith, ... having acknowledged that they were strangers and exiles on the earth" - *xenoi kai parepidemoi*). There are also two references in the Greek Old Testament (the Septuagint) which are clearly the source of the three New Testament occurences. These are Genesis 23:4, the words of Abraham to the sons of Heth, "A sojourner and a stranger (*paroikos kai parepidemos)* am I among you"; and Psalm 39:12 where David says, "O Lord, hearken to my prayer ... for I am a sojourner (*paroikos*) in the land and a stranger, (*parepidemos)* as all my fathers were."

The last of the three words, *diaspora,* likewise occurs twice again in the New Testament: John 7:35, where the Pharisees cynically inquire "Does he intend to go the the Dispersion among the Greeks and teach the Greeks?"; and at the beginning of James's epistle: "James ... to the twelve tribes in the Dispersion: Greeting."

According to *The New International Dictionary of New Testament Theology,* Vol.1, p.685, "The Greek word has 3 different meanings (1) the event or state of the dispersion of the Jews among heathen nations (Deuteronomy 28:25; Jeremiah 34:17 = 41:17 *LXX*); (2) the community of those so dispersed among the Gentiles (Isaiah 49:6; Psalm 147:2; 2 Maccabees 1:27; Pss. Sol. 8:28); (3) the place or country where the scattered Jews now live (Judith 5:19; Test. Ass.7:2)."

That Peter's first epistle was addressed to a Jewish readership could hardly be more clearly stated. And this of course agrees with the fact that Peter had been entrusted with the gospel of the Circumcision. James, Cephas and John gave to Paul and Barnabas the right hand of fellowship, that these (Paul and Barnabas) should go to the nations and they to the circumcision - see Galatians 2:7-10. This solemn agreement is meaningless unless the two parties were faithful to their respective missions. It is of course true that Peter was the first one to open the door to the Gentiles when the Lord sent him to Cornelius. But this event was *before* the agreement with Paul in Galatians 2:9. There was at that time no Gentile mission (and no agreement), and consequently the Lord saw fit to send Peter, the apostle who had the most influence and authority over the believers in Jerusalem, who were the ones most likely to object to Gentiles.

In view of these facts it is all the more remarkable that virtually every recent (and not so recent) commentator and critic is united in the view that 1 Peter is addressed to a predominantly Gentile readership! They argue that the Jewish terms "sojourners" and "dispersion" are here transferred to the Christian church (Gentiles as well as Jews) on the grounds that the church is the New Israel and has accordingly taken over the terms and titles applicable to Israel. Some of the reasons for adopting this position are stated as follows by Donald Guthrie in his *New Testament Introduction* (p.794).

> "The most damaging criticism of the theory of Jewish addressees is the manner in which the writer appeals to the readers' previously 'vain way of life' (1:18), mentions their 'former lusts in ignorance' (1:14), speaks of them having done what the Gentiles do (4:3,4, then follows a list of Gentile vices), and reminds them that they were once a 'no-people' but were called out of darkness (2:9,10)."

The last "criticism" need not delay us since the passages in Hosea to which the apostle is referring are addressed specifically to *Israel*. Hosea here tells the ten tribes, who were about to go into exile to Assyria, that they were "without mercy" (*Lo-Ruhamah*) and "not my people" (*Lo-Ammi*). Nevertheless, "In the place where it was said to them, 'You are not my people', they will be called 'sons of the living God'" (Hosea 1:10, *NIV*), and "I will show my love to the one I called 'Not-my-loved-one'" (2:23, *NIV*). Writing to some of the places where these Israelites were taken captive, the apostle declares, "Once you were no people but now you are God's people; once you had not received mercy but now you have received mercy" (2:10). How wonderfully appropriate this allusion is in a letter addressed to Jews in territory once ruled by Assyria! This moving fulfilment of Hosea's prophecy among Christian descendants of the ten tribes could not fail to impress them.

As for the rest of Guthrie's "most damaging criticism" (which is also that of other critics), the gist of it is that epithets such as *vanity* and *ignorance* are not applicable to Jewish readers whose religion and "way of life" were the subjects of divine revelation. It is true that "vanity" is a word especially appropriate to Gentiles (see Acts 14:15; Ephesians 4:17); and likewise "ignorance" (Acts 17:30; Ephesians 4:18). But the Jews are also said to be both "vain" (Matthew 15:9; James 1:26; Titus 3:9) and "ignorant" (Acts 3:17; Romans 10:3). Indeed, from the Christian point of view, there was not much to choose between them (for all have sinned and fallen short). Only in Christ could their deep-seated ignorance and vanity be removed.

Guthrie's criticism is in fact answered by himself in the very next paragraph. He there says, "Many of the Jews of the Dispersion were only loosely attached to Judaism, and would have formed, with the Gentile proselytes, a ready audience for the first evangelistic impact of the Christian missions." Proselytes to Judaism would certainly have come within the orbit of Peter's catchment as a fisher of men. On the day of Pentecost the assembled crowd whom Peter addressed consisted of "both Jews and proselytes" (Acts 2:10). The presence of many former Gentiles in the shape of proselytes, in addition to hellenized Jews, is quite sufficient to justify Peter's language in 1 Peter 4:3 - "Let the time that is past suffice for doing what the Gentiles like to do, living in licentiousness, passions, drunkenness, revels, carousing, and lawless idolatry."

E. G. Selwyn, while admitting the validity of this argument, has another objection: "the 'vain conversation' of the readers' life admits of the view that they had been lapsed Jews", nevertheless still holds that "the description of it as 'handed down by tradition of your fathers' could hardly have been used of any but Gentiles."

Selwyn refers to 1 Peter 1:18 where the apostle speaks of "the futile ways inherited from your fathers". Frankly I find it incredible that a responsible commentator should find in this statement an argument for a Gentile readership. The phrase "inherited from your fathers" ("handed down by tradition of your fathers") is one word in the Greek - *patroparadotou*. This word is composed of *pateres*, fathers, and *paradotos*, handed down (by tradition). Surely, of all the things one associates with the Jewish people, *tradition* and *the fathers* are among the first to come to mind. Stephen mentions the fathers no less than 11 times in Acts 7, and the complaint is frequent that the Jews made void the word of God through their traditions (Matthew 15:3,6 etc.).

Although this particular word, *patroparadotos,* is not found elsewhere in the Bible, it bears an uncanny resemblance to Galatians 1:14 where Paul admits to his former zeal "for the tradition of my fathers *(patrikon mou paradoseon)*". Paul's zeal for the tradition of his fathers resulted in his fanatical persecution of believers in Christ, a course of action which he elsewhere ascribes to *ignorance* (1 Timothy 1:13)!

Another argument which is often invoked in this connection is that very few Jews were slaves, and consequently the advice given to slaves in 1 Peter 2:18-21 is out of place in a letter addressed to Jews. But here again they are wide of the mark. The word translated "slaves" in the *NIV* and "servants" in the *RSV* is not the usual word for "slave", namely *doulos* , but the milder word *oiketai* . This word occurs elsewhere in the New Testament only in Luke 16:13, Acts 10:7 and Romans 14:4. It means "household servant, domestic", and has a more general application than *doulos.* Who can say that there were no *oiketai* among the Jewish Christians addressed in this letter?

I conclude therefore that 1 Peter is addressed to believers in Jesus Christ, scattered over a wide area, and drawn initially from the *Jews and proselytes* of the Diaspora in Pontus, Galatia, Cappadocia, Asia, and Bithynia. We believe this to be so, not only because the letter is uneqivocally addressed to this class of person, but more especially because Peter, the apostle to the Circumcision, was not sent to the Gentiles as such. Represented at the feast of Pentecost were (1) the Babylonian Dispersion, where Peter was now working (1 Peter 5:13, see Acts 2:9); (2) the Asiatic Dispersion - Cappadocia, Pontus, and Asia are mentioned in Acts 2:9; (3) the Egyptian Dispersion - "*both Jews and proselytes* " (Acts 2:10). It was natural for Peter to assume responsibilty for those he had been instrumental in converting. So here, in 1 Peter, we find him working among the dispersion in Mesopotamia and writing to the dispersion in Asia.

Peter addressed his letter to potentially a vast area - roughly speaking the whole of Asia Minor north of the Taurus Mountains. In practice however it was probably Galatia proper which is meant and the north-east part of the province of Asia, namely those parts which had not been evangelized by Paul. Paul, it will be recalled, had been forbidden by the Spirit to enter *Bithynia* (Acts 16:7), or to speak the word in *Asia* (16:6). The reason for this is clear. These were precisely the regions which had been reserved for *Peter*. Paul made it his habit to preach the gospel where Christ was not known, so that he would not build on someone else's foundation (Romans 15:20). But Peter had already laid the foundation in Asia and Bithynia (amongst other places) on the day of Pentecost. We find, therefore, Peter going and writing to those areas where there was already a Jewish-Christian community, and Paul working in areas where Christ was not previously known. E.G. Selwyn has this to say:

> "There is nothing, therefore, in the address of 1 Peter to require us to suppose that it was intended to reach churches that were mainly Pauline. There were parts of Galatia and Asia, and important parts too, which St Paul had, so far as we know, not visited; nor does he ever seem to have set foot in Pontus, Cappadocia, or Bithynia. On the other hand, these were districts to which Christianity had spread at a very early date. Three of them - and indeed four, if we may reckon the Phrygia of Acts 2:10 as meaning Galatic rather than Asian Phrygia - were represented among the pilgrims who were present at Pentecost and heard St. Peter interpret that excited scene in his first sermon; and they would have been the earliest

to bring tidings of the new religion to their homes." (See pages 45-6.)

In view of the clear demarcation which separates the sphere of Peter's influence from that of Paul, the insistence by scholars that Peter wrote his letter from *Rome* rather than Babylon seems all the more incongruous. This problem we deal with in the Appendix *By the waters of Babyon.*

Points of Jewish interest

Points of Jewish interest

1 Peter, like all the rest of Scripture, is "inspired by God and profitable for teaching, for reproof, for correction, and for training in righteousness, that the man of God may be complete, equipped for every good work" (2 Timothy 3:16,17). 1 Peter in particular contains many pasages which Christians of every generation have found to be extremely helpful and relevant to them personally. Nevertheless, in an epistle addressed specifically to Jewish readers it would be surprising if certain passages did not address their situation in particular or were couched in language which they alone would appreciate. The following passages seem to fall into these categories.

1 Peter 1:2: "... sanctified by the Spirit for obedience to Jesus Christ and for sprinkling with his blood."

It is only in 1 Peter and Hebrews, both addressed to Jewish Christians, that the words *rhantismos* and *rhantizo*, sprinkling and sprinkle, occur. See Hebrews 9:13,14 "For if the sprinkling of defiled persons with the blood of goats and bulls and with the ashes of a heifer sanctifies for the purification of the flesh, how much more shall the blood of Christ ..."; Hebrews 9:19,20 "For when every commandment of the law had been declared by Moses to all the people, he took the blood of calves and goats, with water and scarlet wool and hyssop, and sprinkled both the book itself and all the people, saying, 'This is the blood of the covenant which God commanded you'"; Hebrews 9:21; 10:22; 12:24.

The people were sprinkled with "the blood of the covenant" at the making of the covenant in Exodus 24:8.

On the day of Atonement the sanctuary and its sacred objects were cleansed by the sprinkling of the blood of a bull or a goat offered as a sin offering, according to Leviticus 16:9-19.

A person suffering from an infectious skin disease, such as leprosy, had to be sprinkled seven times with the blood of a bird - Leviticus 14:1-7.

A Jewish Christian might be expected to understand an allusion to the sprinkling of blood. It would however have been lost on a Gentile believer. He might even be forgiven for thinking that the allusion was to the rites of Mithras, in which the votaries descended into a pit where the blood of a bull dripped on them through a grid! *He* might be forgiven, but not R. Perdelwitz who has made the same suggestion in recent times!

1 Peter 1:17: "conduct yourselves with fear throughout the time of your exile *(paroikias)*."

1 Peter 2:11: "Beloved, I beseech you as aliens *(paroikous)* and exiles to abstain from the passions of the flesh that wage war against your soul."

The second passage is an allusion, as we have seen, to Genesis 23:4 or Psalm 39:12 where the same two words occur. *Paroikia* and *paroikoi* are the words normally translated "sojourn" and "sojourners" in the older translations of the Bible. Where they occur in the New Testament they usually contain a reference to the history of Israel. So Acts 7:6 refers to Genesis 15:13; Acts 7:29 to Exodus 2:15; Acts 13:17 to Exodus 6:6; Hebrews 11:9 to passages in Genesis relating to Abraham; Hebrews 11:13 to Genesis 23:4.

In 1 Peter it is natural to see a reference to the status of dispersed Israel as resident aliens in the countries of their exile. But this does not have to be the case since, in Ephesians 2:19, Gentile believers are said to be "no longer strangers and sojourners (*xenoi kai paroikoi)*" but "fellow citizens with the saints and members of the household of God."   Previously the Gentiles had been strangers to the covenants of promise (v.12) or at best affiliated aliens, but now, says the apostle, they are "fellow citizens with the saints" and complete members of the new household of which Ephesians speaks.

1 Peter 1:12: "It was revealed to them (the prophets) that they were serving not themselves but *you*."

This makes a lot more sense if the Christians addressed in 1 Peter were the direct descendants of those whom the prophets originally spoke to. While addressing the Israelites of their own day, the prophets are often looking ahead to a future generation rather than their own contemporaries.

One of the most remarkable features of 1 Peter is the abundance of quotations from, and allusions to, the Old Testament. This would surely indicate a readership which was thoroughly familiar with the Old Testament scriptures. Moreover, most of the quotations are from the Septuagint which was the Bible of Greek speaking Jews.

1 Peter 1:18,19: "You know that you were ransomed from the futile ways inherited from your fathers, not with perishable things such as silver or gold, but with the precious blood of Christ, like that of a lamb without blemish or spot."

It is only in books addressed to Jewish believers that Christ is referred to as a lamb (*amnos*). John the Baptist, when he saw Jesus approaching, exclaimed "Behold, the Lamb of God, who takes away the sin of the world!" (John 1:29). And the Ethiopian eunuch, reading from Isaiah 53, recited, "As a sheep led to the slaughter or a lamb before its shearer is dumb, so he opens not his mouth" (Acts 8:32).

The synonymous word *arnion* is used of Christ 28 times in the book of Revelation, and once of the the Beast out of the earth who "had two horns like a lamb and it spoke like a dragon" (Revelation 13:11). It is found also in John 21:15 where Jesus says to Simon Peter, "Feed my lambs."

In the Septuagint *amnos* is used frequently in sacrificial contexts, and this is true of the few New Testament references as well. On the other hand, *arnion* is very rare in the Septuagint.

A partial exception to the above may be 1 Corinthians 5:7 where, in the context of purging out the old leaven, the apostle says, "For Christ, our paschal lamb (literally "our passover"), has been sacrificed." He is evidently addressing believers who were familiar with the Passover and the details of its observance and 1 Corinthians 5:1 suggests that in this passage Paul has in mind the Jewish Christians in Corinth. There is however no word for "lamb" in this passage.

1 Peter 2:4,5: "Come to him, to that living stone, rejected by men but in God's sight chosen and precious; and like living stones be yourselves built into a spiritual house, to be a holy priesthood, to offer spiritual sacrifices acceptable to God through Jesus Christ."

This whole section, verses 4-8, is based on a number of Old Testament allusions. Psalm 118:22 ("The stone which the builders rejected has become the head of the corner - quoted in v.7); Exodus 19:6 ("you shall be to me a kingdom of priests and a holy nation" - compare v.9 "a royal priesthood"); Isaiah 28:16 ("Behold, I am laying in Zion for a foundation a stone, a tested stone, a precious cornerstone, of a sure foundation: He who believes will not be in haste" - quoted in v.6); and Isaiah 8:14 ("And he will become a sanctuary, and a stone of offence, and a rock of stumbling to both houses of Israel, a trap and a snare to the inhabitants of Jerusalem" - quoted in v.8).

There is also an allusion to Isaiah 28:16 in Ephesians 2:20 where the same word for "cornerstone" appears. In this pasage the Church of today is said to be built on the foundation of the apostles and prophets (the same as those to whom the mystery had been revealed, 3:5), and the whole structure is *growing* into a holy temple in the Lord. The two temples are quite distinct. There is nevertheless a superficial similarity between 1 Peter 2:5 ("you yourselves as living stones are being built, *oikodomeisthe*, into a spiritual house for a holy priesthood") and Ephesians 2:22 ("in whom you also are being built together, *sunoikodomeisthe*, into a dwelling place of God by the Spirit").

One might also compare 1 Corinthians 3:16, "Do you not know that you are God's temple and that God's Spirit dwells in you?" and 2 Corinthians 6:16, "For we are the temple of the living God." Several human temples seem to be in view, one of them consisting of the redeemed of Israel in the future. This temple was already taking shape among those to whom Peter was ministering.

1 Peter 2:9: "But you are a chosen race, a royal priesthood, a holy nation, God's own people, that you may declare the wonderful deeds of him who called you out of darkness into his marvellous light."

We have here a combination of Exodus 19:6 (*Septuagint*) and Isaiah 43:20,21 (*Septuagint* with modifications), with a sidewards glance at Malachi 3:17.

> Exodus 19:6 - "and you shall be to me a royal priesthood and a holy nation (*basileion hierateuma kai ethnos hagion*)."

> Isaiah 43:20,21 - "I have given water in the wilderness, and rivers in the dry land, to give drink to my chosen race (*genos mou to eklekton*), even my people whom I have preserved (*laon mou hon periepoisamen*) to tell forth my praises."
>
> Malachi 3:17 - "And they shall be mine, says the Lord Almighty, in the day which I appoint, for a peculiar possession (*eis peripoiesin*)."

On this passage and 1 Peter 2:5 is based the doctrine of "the priesthood of all believers". But those who propagate this idea fail to notice that each expression used applies only to Israel, in language addressed by the Lord to His chosen nation. The church of today is neither a race, nor a priesthood, nor a nation, and only confusion is created by pretending that it is. Only with respect to being a "peculiar possession" do these words apply to the church (see Ephesians 1:14).

The promise that Israel would be a kingdom of priests and a holy nation was dependent on their total obedience and observance of the covenant. This condition was never fulfilled, and consequently the promise never came to fruition. It is however repeated in

Isaiah 61:6 and its fulfilment declared in Revelation 1:6; 5:10. Israel will yet be a kingdom of priests when they rule with Christ for the duration of His millennial reign. By anticipation believers among the Jews in the Acts period were assured that they already belonged to this elect company.

For a more extended discussion, see *How to Enjoy the Bible* by E.W. Bullinger, pages 125-27.

1 Peter 2:10: "Once you were no people but now you are God's people; once you had not received mercy but now you have received mercy."

It is true that Paul applies this passage from Hosea (1:10) to Gentile believers in Romans 9:24-26, for they also had been "no people" in God's sight but were now "God's people". However, in its original context, as we have already seen, this prophecy is addressed to Israel in captivity. Hosea had said, "in the place where it was said to them, 'You are not my people,' it shall be said to them, 'Sons of the living God.'" Writing to descendants of these very exiles, in some of the places where they had gone, Peter says, "Once you were no people, but now you are God's people." It cannot be denied these words are singularly appropriate in a letter addressed to Jews of the Dispersion in northern Asia.

1 Peter 2:25: "For you were straying like sheep, but have now returned to the Shepherd and Guardian of your souls."

It is only in books addressed to Jewish believers that Christ is referred to as Shepherd. See Matthew 26:31 (=Mark 14:27); John 10:11,14,16; Hebrews 13:20; 1 Peter 5:4. Likewise it is the house of Israel which is called "lost sheep" (Matthew 10:6; 15:24; John

10 *passim*). However the nations are also designated sheep in Matthew 25:33 and pastors are really "shepherds" in Ephesians 4:11. Believers are "the flock" in Acts 20:28 and it is the job of "guardians" (overseers, bishops) to "shepherd" the church of God. In the passage before us (1 Peter 2:24,25) Peter is quoting from Isaiah 53, verses 5,6 and 12 - "with his stripes we are healed. All we like sheep have gone astray; we have turned every one to his own way... yet he bore the sin of many."

It was to Peter that the Lord said three times "Feed my lambs", "Feed my sheep" (John 21:15-17). It is this ministry which he is fulfilling in his two epistles. He even instructs the elders, as a fellow elder, to do the same. Literally, "Shepherd the flock of God which is among you, not by compulsion but willingly according to God, nor from desire for gain but eagerly, nor as exercising lordship over the lost but by becoming examples to the flock, and when the chief Shepherd appears you will receive the unfading crown of glory" (5:1-4).

1 Peter 3:6: "... as Sarah obeyed Abraham, calling him lord. And you are now (literally *became*) her children if you do right and let nothing terrify you."

According to Kelly the choice of the word "became" implies that they were formerly pagans since, if they were Jews, they would have no need to *become* Sarah's daughters! But true pedigree is based on character, not ancestry (Matthew 5:45; John 8:39; Galatians 3:29). This verse does not prove that the ones addressed were physical daughters of Sarah, but it may nevertheless be implied. If they want to be *true* children of Sarah, he is saying, in deed as well as name they should behave as Sarah did. Like Sarah they should adorn themselves "with the imperishable jewel of a gentle and quiet spirit", not with the outward adorning of gold, fine clothes and plaiting of the hair! They should moreover be submissive to their husbands and do what is right without fear.

There are doubtless several other passages which could be quoted as being of special interest to Jewish Christians. But we now move on to an examination of Peter's theology to see how it compares with that of Paul.

Recurring themes

Recurring themes

Re-birth

The theme of **Re-birth** is not over prominent in 1 Peter, it is nevertheless a theme which recurs a few times. In fact it is only in 1 Peter that the verb *anagennao*, to be born again, occurs at all in the New Testament. Paul never describes conversion in terms of being born again, though twice he speaks of having *begotten* some folk through the gospel, namely the Corinthians in 1 Corinthians 4:15 and Onesimus in Philemon 10. In these places he refers to himself as the spiritual father of those he has brought to Christ.

Apart from Peter, it is the apostle John, in his gospel and first epistle, who lays stress on the concept of re-birth. It occurs in John 1:13 ("who were born, not of blood nor of the will of the flesh nor of the will of man, but of God"), and in the story of Nicodemus (John 3:1-8). Re-birth is something only God can do; all human participation is for ever removed. It is therefore a very expressive picture of the radical change which takes place when a person puts his faith in Christ for salvation.

1 Peter 1:3: "By his great mercy we have been born anew to a living hope through the resurrection of Jesus Christ from the dead."

1:23: "You have been born anew, not of perishable seed but of imperishable, through the living and abiding word of God."

2:2: "Like newborn babes, long for the pure spiritual milk, that by it you may grow up to salvation."

Hope

Considerably more prominent is the theme of *hope*. It is not only an inheritance, kept in heaven, for which they wait, but salvation itself, a salvation ready to be revealed in the last time, at the revelation of Jesus Christ. Paul, during the Acts period, also speaks of this future salvation when he says, "For salvation is nearer to us now than when we first believed; the night is far gone, the day is at hand" (Romans 13:11,12). For Peter too "the end of all things is at hand" (4:7). Hence the urgency we sense in this epistle.

1 Peter 1:3-7: "By his great mercy we have been born anew to a living hope through the resurrection of Jesus Christ from the dead, and to an inheritance which is imperishable, undefiled, and unfading, kept in heaven for you, who by God's power are guarded through faith for a salvation ready to be revealed in the last time ... at the revelation of Jesus Christ."

1:9-10: "As the outcome of your faith you obtain the salvation of your souls. The prophets who prophesied of the grace that was to be yours searched and inquired about this salvation..."

1:13: "Therefore gird up your minds, be sober, set your hope fully upon the grace that is coming to you at the revelation of Jesus Christ."

1:21: "Through him you have confidence in God, who raised him from the dead and gave him glory, so that your faith and hope are in God."

Rejoicing

Peter has this in common with Paul, the ability to rejoice! Like Paul he rejoices not only in spite of his suffering, but even because of them. However, the verb he uses, *agalliao*, to exult, is nowhere to be found in Paul's writings.

1 Peter 1:6: "In this (the salvation ready to be revealed in the last time) you rejoice, though now for a little while you may have to suffer various trials..."

1:8: "though you do not now see him you believe in him and rejoice with unutterable and exalted joy."

4:13: "But rejoice in so far as you share Christ's sufferings, that you may also rejoice and be glad when his glory is revealed."

Suffering

Suffering, especially Christ's suffering on our behalf, is one of the principal themes of this epistle. Suffering however is constantly linked with glory, the glory to be revealed at the second coming of Christ.

1 Peter 1:11: "They (the prophets) inquired what person or time was indicated by the Spirit of Christ within them when predicting the sufferings of Christ and the subsequent glory."

2:21: "For to this (suffering) you have been called, because Christ also suffered for you, leaving you an example, that you should follow in his steps."

4:1: "Since therefore Christ suffered in the flesh, arm yourselves with the same thought, for whoever has suffered in the flesh has ceased from sin."

4:13: "But rejoice in so far as you share Christ's sufferings, that you may also rejoice and be glad when his glory is revealed."

5:1: "So I exhort the elders among you, as a fellow elder and a witness of the sufferings of Christ as well as a partaker in the glory that is to be revealed."

It is clear from some of these passages that persecution had already begun. This is further proved by the following. It is emphasised in many of them that their trials are for the purpose of testing, and that approval and blessing may be expected if they are endured patiently.

1 Peter 1:6-7: "now for a little while you may have to suffer various trials, so that the genuineness of your faith, more precious than gold which though perishable is tested by fire, may redound to praise and glory and honour at the revelation of Jesus Christ."

2:19-20: "For one is approved if, mindful of God, he endures pain while suffering unjustly.... But if when you do right and suffer for it you take it patiently, you have God's approval."

3:14: "But even if you do suffer for righteousness' sake, you will be blessed. Have no fear of them, nor be troubled."

3:16-17: "and keep your conscience clear, so that, when you are abused, those who revile your good behaviour in Christ may be put to shame. For it is better to suffer for doing right, if that should be God's will, than for doing wrong."

4:12: "Beloved, do not be surprised at the fiery ordeal which comes upon you to prove you, as though something strange were happening to you."

4:14-17: "If you are reproached for the name of Christ, you are blessed, because the spirit of glory and of God rests upon you.... if one suffers as a Christian, let him not be ashamed, but under that name let him glorify God. For the time has come for judgment to begin with the household of God."

4:19: "Therefore let those who suffer according to God's will do right and entrust their souls to a faithful Creator."

5:9-10: "Resist him (the devil), firm in your faith, knowing that the same experience of suffering is required of your brotherhood throughout the world. And after you have suffered a little while, the God of all grace, who has called you to his eternal glory in Christ, will himself restore, establish, and strengthen you."

But Christ's sufferings are not simply an example to be followed. First and foremost they are the means of redemption, and it is by faith in his blood that we are saved. This is also made clear in this epistle.

1 Peter 1:18-19: "You know that you were ransomed from the futile ways inherited from your fathers, not with perishable things such as silver or gold, but with the precious blood of Christ, like that of a lamb without blemish or spot."

2:24: "He himself bore our sins in his body on the tree, that we might die to sin and live to righteousness. By his wounds you have been healed."

3:18: "For Christ also died for sins once for all, the righteous for the unrighteous, that he might bring us to God, being put to death in the flesh but made alive in the spirit.; in which he went and preached to the spirits in prison ..."

There is no need for me to comment on "the spirits in prison" seeing that Bullinger's definitive exposition is again in print (OBT, 1999). It is noteworthy, however, that J.N.D. Kelly, by a rigorous application of Biblical principles, has arrived at much the same interpretation as Bullinger in both 3:18-20 and 4:6. This may be seen as a welcome confirmation of what we believe to be the truth. Other commentators continue to indulge in fanciful speculation.

Conclusion

Conclusion

If we are to rightly divide and understand the Word of Truth it is important to distinguish between those writings addressed primarily to a Jewish audience and those addressed to Gentiles as well as Jewish Christians. James, Peter and John are foremost among those sent to the Circumcision (Galatians 3:9), and the epistles written by them are to be found in that order in our Bibles. The Lord Jesus was Himself "a minister to the Circumcision" ((Romans 15:8) so far as His earthly ministry was concerned, and all twelve apostles fall into this category.

Paul and Barnabas, on the other hand, were chief among those who were sent to the nations (Galatians 3:9). We need however, to distinguish between Paul's earlier ministry "to the Jew first" from his later ministry to a predominantly Gentile audience in the post-Acts period. That however is not the subject of this treatise.

In this booklet I have endeavoured to isolate those aspects of 1 Peter which point to its Jewish provenance and character. It only remains to decide whether it was written from Babylon or Rome. Since some readers may not feel this to be an improtant issue, I have put my comments in the following Appendix.

But more important than the above consideration is the inducement to holy living, patience under suffering, and love for one's neighbour. Only by reading the epistle right through can its overall message and relevance for today be fully appreciated.

Appendix:
By the waters
of Babylon

Appendix: By the waters of Babylon

We now turn to the end of 1 Peter, to those who send greetings. We read in 1 Peter 5:13 (*NIV*), "She who is in Babylon, chosen together with you, sends you her greetings, and so does my son Mark." This has given rise to much speculation. Some have thought that Peter's wife is meant, and his son born to her - Mark! Most however have realised that the Greek contains an ellipse or lacuna. Literally - "The ... in Babylon, co-chosen, sends you greetings."

What is needed is a feminine noun to agree with the feminine article *the*. It is hardly surprising that most commentators have plumped for the word *ekklesia*, church. Here is a feminine noun which exactly fits the bill - "the *church* in Babylon sends you greetings." There is however one small problem which the commentators have overlooked. An ellipse must always be supplied from the context. *Ekklesia*, however, occurs nowhere in this epistle at all!

In point of fact, as Bullinger pointed out years ago, the feminine noun required is not *ekklesia* but *diaspora*. The word *diaspora* has to be supplied from the opening verse: this epistle is addressed to the *diaspora* in Pontus etc. and sent from the *diaspora* in Babylon. Moreover, the diaspora in Babylon was "co-elect" with those to whom the letter is addressed. As Bishop Wordsworth says, "The preposition *sun* (co-) is a link which connects the elect at Babylon with the elect in Asia." Dr. John Lightfoot made the same point back in 1658. He had this to say:

"As for the word 'church,' it is not in the original, but only *he en Babuloni suneklekte.* But translations generally say, 'church:' and I know not what word else could come in, unless *diaspora* 'the dispersion,' used ver. 1, of the Epistle: and then there is this parity. They, to whom he writes, are *diaspora,* and *eklektoi,* the 'dispersion,' and the 'elected;' and so are these, among whom he is." (Pitman edition, Vol. VII, p.8)

Lightfoot and Wordsworth would allow *ekklesia* as well as *diaspora.* But in our view *diaspora* is alone admissible, because *diaspora* is the only word which can be validated from the context. As for Mark, he is doubtless John Mark in whose house Peter had been a familiar visitor (Acts 12:12-17).

It is clearly stated that this epistle was written from *Babylon.* But, once again, our scholars, with amazing unanimity, are certain that literal Babylon cannot be seriously entertained. No, they affirm that what is meant is not Babylon on the Euphrates, but the Babylon on the Tiber, the capital city of the monstrous empire which then ruled the world. As for the reason for this cryptic reference to Rome, scholars are divided. Some think it was for security reasons that Peter wished to hide his true whereabouts. As Guthrie explains, "At the time of writing, Rome was the centre of vicious actions against Christianity and avoidance of any mention of the Roman church would be a wise move if the letter fell into official hands."

But others have felt that this is farfetched. After all Paul felt no such qualms (Romans 1:7,15; 2 Timothy 1:17), and Peter insists on obedience to the emperor (1 Peter 2:13-17). A better suggestion is that the motive is homiletic - Babylon being employed as a symbol for the spiritual exile of Christians in the world. There is indeed a profound homiletic significance in the name Babylon. This was the place where the exiles first went, and was almost synonymous with the exile itself. But the allusion is far more poignant if the literal Babylon is meant rather than a poorly-concealed cypher for somewhere else. The very mention of Babylon conjures up all the tearful sentiments of Psalm 137:1-6:

> "By the waters of Babylon, there we sat down and wept, when we remembered Zion. ... If I forget you, O Jerusalem, let my right hand wither! Let my tongue cleave to the roof of my mouth, if I do not remember you, if I do not set Jerusalem above my highest joy!"

Guthrie is representative of scholarly opinion on the subject of Babylon. He objects to the Babylonian provenance of 1 Peter for the following reasons:

> "(1) Peter is nowhere else associated with this region; (2) the Eastern Church did not until a late period claim any association with Peter in its Church origins; (3) the area itself was very sparsely populated, especially in the period subsequent to the migration in AD 41 (cf. Josephus, *Antiquities*, XVIII. 9.8) and the resultant massacre of large numbers of Jews in Seleucia; (4) early tradition centred the activities of Peter in the West and not the East; (5) Mark almost certainly found a sphere of activity in the West, but nothing is known of him working in the East." (pp. 801,2)

Scholars are very quick to point out the weakness of traditional associations of Peter with Babylon. They are far less keen to point out the equally weak traditions associating Peter with Rome! If it is tradition which is felt to settle the matter, let us for a moment examine the tradition that Peter laboured in Rome.

The whole question of Peter's residence and martyrdom in Rome is discussed with great candour by Oscar Cullmann in *Peter: Disciple, Apostle, Martyr* (1953). Cullmann is anxious to prove that Peter *did* go to Rome and was martyred there. He leans over backwards to extract the faintest inference from the meagre evidence available. He is nevertheless commendably honest in his final appraisal. In order to correct the balance on the question of tradition, I include here his own summing up. The italics are his, not mine.

> "*Prior to the second half of the second century no document asserts explicitly the stay and martyrdom of Peter in Rome.....* As far as his *activity* in the Roman church is concerned, no early text compels us to contest it. But on the other hand, neither is it explicitly mentioned by a single text of the ancient period, and in any case it is difficult, for reasons of chronology, to include a very long activity. Of an episcopal office of Peter nothing is ever said. In the form in which this office is first attested in the fourth century, it is historically impossible.... As far as the *martyr death of Peter in Rome* is concerned, we have concerning it two texts that must be regarded as indirect witnesses: 1 Clement, ch.5, and Ignatius, Romans 4:3. Neither of them says explicitly that Peter had been in Rome." (pp. 113,4)

In the middle of the second century we have the extensive writings of Justin Martyr who actually lived in Rome. But neither in his *Apologies* nor in the *Dialogue with Trypho* is Peter's stay in Rome ever mentioned. However, in the second half of the second century the traditions concerning Peter's residence in Rome begin to proliferate. In increasing numbers they assert that Peter was in Rome and was martyred there. On the reliability of these late texts Cullmann has this to say:

> "In theory the possibility cannot be excluded that perhaps here and there the basis of the tradition is a good early source which we no longer possess. Yet even if this is so, we must be fundamentally sceptical towards these late texts, when we see how in this very period the development of Christian legend flourishes and how it seeks to fill out the gaps in the New Testament narrative." (p.115)

Cullmann does not stand alone. Another writer who thinks the tradition of Peter's residence in Rome should be regarded with scepticism is Michael Grant (in *Saint Peter*, 1994, pp.147-9). Grant gives eight cogent reasons why this tradition should be questioned, but keeps an open mind himself. We may be sure that Peter was not in Rome all the while that Paul was writing letters to and from that city, or he would doubtless have received a mention. But in view of the strong body of tradition that Peter was martyred in Rome, it would be hazardous to insist that he never went there. All that I have any wish to demonstrate is that Peter was not in Rome when he wrote his first epistle.

If I have to choose between two equally weak traditions, only one of which has the support of the Bible, I know which to choose! Four of Guthrie's arguments are in fact appeals to tradition. This leaves only one - the allegation that the area (Babylon) was very sparsely populated in the period subsequent to the migration in AD 41 and the resultant massacre of large numbers of Jews in Seleucia.

Josephus, in the place mentioned (*Antiquities of the Jews* XVIII, 9.8,9), speaks of warfare between the Babylonians and the Jews, resulting in the migration of the latter to Seleucia, the principal city of those parts. There, however, the Greeks and Syrians fell upon the Jews and slew about 50,000 of them - "nay, the Jews were all destroyed, excepting a few who escaped." He goes on to relate that "the whole nation of the Jews" were so much in fear that "most of them gathered themselves together, and went to Neerda and Nisibis, and obtained security there by the strength of those cities."

There was therefore still a "nation of the Jews" in Babylonia even after the massacre of some 50,000 in Seleucia which all but wiped out that particular enclave. Other writers dilate on the large numbers of Jews residing in that area. Among these are Josephus and Philo, both contemporaries. According to Josephus, "there were not a few ten thousands of this people that had been carried captives, and dwelt about Babylonia" (*Antiquities of the Jews* XV, 3.1). Dr. Lightfoot has this to say:

> "Babylon was one of the greatest knots (centres) of Jews in the world ... Need I show, how there were multitudes of Jews in Babylon, that returned not with Ezra? Need I tell you, that in that country there were three Jewish universities? Or, need I speak, how there were ten tribes scattered in Assyria? Then how proper was it for Peter to have been there!"

So much for the objections afforded by tradition and history against Peter residing in Babylon. But what, it may be asked, are the positive reasons for taking Babylon literally in 1 Peter 5:13? First and foremost is the simple fact that this is how it is written.

Surely "Babylon" must mean Babylon short of some overriding reason for understanding it otherwise. Wordsworth, who gives the best defence that I have seen, wisely says:

> "Tropes [words or phrases used metaphorically] are scarcely admissible in dates, especially in Epistles like the present, which is remarkable for its quiet tone. In details of fact, the *literal* meaning seems to be the true one, and if the literal meaning will stand, it ought not to be abandoned for a metaphorical one."

That says it all! Tropes, that is figures of speech, are scarcely admissible in dates! Even in the book of Revelation which is always cited as an obvious case where Babylon stands for Rome, it is far from certain that this is the case. In my view Babylon means Babylon even in the book of Revelation, and if that is true in a book like Revelation, how much more so in a book like 1 Peter! Dean Alford is of the same opinion as Wordsworth. He has this to say:

> ".... there does not appear to be any reason to depart from the *prima facie* impression given by this notice, that St. Peter was at that time dwelling and working at the renowned Babylon on the Euphrates.... And it is now generally recognized among Commentators that we are not to find an allegorical meaning in a proper name thus simply used in the midst of simple and matter-of-fact sayings." (Vol. IV, Part 1, p.128)

According to Richard Heard, the absence of any tradition connecting Peter with Babylon may be explained by the great break between the Christian communities of the East and West following AD 70 and the subsequent misadventures of

Christianity in Palestine and elsewhere (*An Introduction to the New Testament,* 1950, p.171). Adolph Schlatter writes, "To an apostle who knew he had been sent to Israel and who, therefore, had to begin with Jerusalem as his headquarters, there was no other part of the Diaspora, once Jerusalem and Galilee were out of the question, which offered greater scope than Babylon" (*The Church in the New Testament Period,* 1955, p.254). If Rome was the centre of the Gentile world, Babylon, after the fall of Jerusalem, was the centre of the Jewish world.

This point of view was "generally recognised among commentators" at the time of Dean Alford and later. Why, therefore, does virtually every commentator take the opposite view today? The evidence has not changed, but very clearly the *fashion* has. No-one likes to be 'out of fashion', and scholars, for all their vaunted objectivity, are no exception. Today it is fashionable to believe that 1 Peter was written from Rome to a predominantly Gentile audience. But the Scriptural pointers are that he wrote from Babylon to a predominantly Jewish audience. It is better surely to follow the Scriptural evidence than the passing fashions of scholarly opinions.

Another argument is as follows. It is a reasonable assumption that the districts enumerated in the opening verse are given in the order in which the courier would have visited them. Wordsworth (following Bengel) makes much of the fact that Pontus, the most *eastern* region, is mentioned first. If Peter had been writing from Rome, "he would not have begun his enumeration with the most distant eastern district, and have proceeded, as he does, in a *westerly* direction, till he ends with *Bythinia*; but he would have reversed the order." Dean Alford makes the same point.

It is doubtful however whether this argument holds water. According to F.J.A. Hort,

> "Babylon lies to the south as well as to the east of Asia Minor, and the northernmost region of Asia Minor is Pontus. The next two names in the list add to the incongruity: the order Pontus, Galatia, Cappadocia is an exact inversion of the order which would present itself to a writer looking mentally towards Asia Minor from Babylon. The appeal to geography therefore in this elementary form, that is, the appeal to mere position on the map, condemns Rome and Babylon alike: in other words, the arrangement of the list must be either accidental or dependent on some different principle." (*The First Epistle of Peter, 1:1-2:17,* 1898, p.168)

He concludes that the courier (Silvanus probably), for reasons which can only be guessed at, started his round journey at Pontus. No help can be derived from the order in which the places are mentioned as to where the epistle was sent from.

It needs to be remembered that Peter was not a young man. In fact he may have been getting on for 70 by the time he wrote 1 Peter. Where, I would ask, are we more likely to find him - labouring among the rude masses in the metropolis, or ministering to his own countrymen (many of whom were already Christians) in Babylon and the eastern provinces? Surely the second alternative is far more in keeping with his age and apostleship.

Finally I would draw attention again to the singular appropriateness of Babylon as the sphere of Peter's activity. Here he was working among people many of whom he had himself converted on the day of Pentecost - just as he was writing to others who were there also. He was moreover in territory untouched by Paul, whereas in Rome he would have been trespassing on Paul's domain. Dr. Lightfoot makes the same point.

> "Peter was the minister of circumcision: and what had he to do at Rome, the chief city of the Gentiles? Paul was there justly; but if Peter had been there, he would have been in Paul's line. Herein, he held agreement with Paul, Galatians 2:9. He with James and John, gave to Paul and Barnabas the right hand of fellowship, that these should go unto the heathen, - and they, unto the circumcision. It is true, there were some Jews in Rome; but they were but a handful in comparison, not a fit company to engage the minister of the circumcision to come thither, to live and die there: but rather on the contrary. But Babylon was one of the greatest knots of Jews in the world...."

Bibliography

Henry Alford, *The Greek Testament*, Vol. IV, Part 1 (Rivingtons, 1861)

Oscar Cullman, *Peter: Disciple, Apostle, Martyr*. Translated from the German by Floyd V. Filson (SCM, 1962)

Edward G. Selwyn, *The First Epistle of St. Peter* (Macmillan, 1949)

Donald Guthrie, *New Testament Introduction* (One volume edition, IVP 1970)

J.N.D. Kelly, *A Commentary of the Epistles of Peter and Jude* (Adam & Charles Black, 1969)

John Lightfoot, *The Whole Works of the late Rev. John Lightfoot, D.D.* Volume VII, pages 1-14, "The Church at Babylon". Edited by John Roger Pitman, (London, 1822)

Christopher Wordsworth, *The Greek Testament with Introduction, Notes and Index*. (Rivingtons, 1961)

Also on this subject

1 Peter was written during the time covered by the Acts of the Apostles. It was a time when an important distinction existed between believers in Christ: were you a Jew or were you a Gentile? Such differences no longer matter, but they did then. If you have found what has been said in this booklet interesting, helpful or challenging, and would like to learn more about just exactly what God was doing during the Acts Period, the following publications will be of interest and help.

Paul's Three Ministries by Michael Penny
A clear and simple explanation of the ministry of Paul, during the book of Acts and afterwards. During Acts, Paul had two distinct ministries, one to the Gentiles and one to the people of Israel (Acts 9:19). What was common to these two ministries, and what was different? Paul's third ministry came after the end of Acts, after all differences between Christian Jews and Christian Gentiles were removed.

The Speeches in Acts by W M Henry
Have you ever noticed how different are the great speeches recorded in the Acts of the Apostles? There are Peter's speeches to the Jews and his ones in relation to Gentiles. There is Stephen's speech to the Sanhedrin and James' speech to the Jewish Apostles and Elders. Then there are Paul's speeches to Jews and God-fearing Gentiles, and also the one to the Pagans in Athens. Why are some so similar to each other? But why are some so different?

God's Grand Design by Charles Ozanne

So precisely what was going on in the Acts of the Apostles? One of the best commentaries on the Acts Period, and God's different dealings with the Jews and Gentiles of that time, is Romans chapters 9 to 11. Here we discover His unsearchable ways, marvel at His inscrutable judgments, and gain a greater appreciation of His divine mercy.

Think on these things

By Ernest Streets

Think on these things deals with many subjects relating to the time covered by the Acts of the Apostles, and to the Jews and Gentiles of that time. Ernest Streets has some distinctive insights which readers will find answer many questions. The subjects covered include .....

- Paul's ministry,
- The believer's hope,
- The Gospel of Salvation,
- The Gospel of John, Understanding the Bible,
- The Body of Christ,
- Mark 16:17,
- The Lord's Supper,
- The Covenants,
- The last 12 verses of Mark's Gospel,
- The churches and the Church,
- The mystery of the gospel,
- God's eternal purpose
- ..... and more.

Think on these things,
**and the other publications mentioned in this book
can be obtined from**

www.obt.org.uk

and from

**The Open Bible Trust
Fordland Mount,. Upper Basildon,
Reading, RG8 8LU, UK.**

**They are also available as eBooks from Amazon and Apple
and as a KDP paperback from Amazon.**

About the author

Charles Ozanne was born in Crowborough, Sussex, in 1936. He read Theology at Oxford before undertaking research in the book of Revelation for his PhD at the University of Manchester under F. F. Bruce. Some of his recent publications for the Open Bible Trust have been a commentary on Daniel, entitled *Empires of the End-Time;* a critique of Replacement Theology entitled *God's Plan for Israel: Replacement or Restoration?* And a work looking at *The Sabbath and Circumcision.* A major work, *The Believer's Guide to Bible Chronology* has been published by *Authorhouse.* however, it is available from the Open Bible Trust.

Another major work is *Understanding the New Testament.* A well-written and well-presented commentary on the whole of the New Testament, showing that each of the 27 documents, although distinctive, fit into an overall pattern. For further details of this latest book, and others, please visit **www.obt.org.uk**

Charles Ozanne's work on *God's Plan for Israel* is avaialble as an eBook fromn Amazon and Apple.

Also by Charles Ozanne

Other works by Charles Ozanne published by the Open Bible Trust include:

That you may believe – the eight signs of John's Gospel
The word of the Kingdom – in Matthew's Gospel
Nahum's Vision Concerning Nineveh
That you may be filled – Ephesians
God's grand design – Romans 9-11
Malachi: The Lord's Messenger
The Pastorals in Perspective
The priority of Philippians
Baptism – rite and reality
Esther and Ruth, Joshua-Jesus

For a full list, and for details of the above, please visit

www.obt.org.uk

About this book

Introducing 1 Peter

This booklet is not a commentary on 1 Peter, but simply an introduction, in which the author has tried to answer such questions as …

- to whom it was written,
- where it was written from,
- why was it witten.

He also gives a brief survey of its character and contents.

There are already many useful conmmentaries in existence, but this booklet meets head on, and hopefully answers convincingly, a few questions on which some commentators avoid, questions of particular relevance to students of the Bible.

Publications of The Open Bible Trust must be in accordance with its evangelical, fundamental and dispensational basis. However, beyond this minimum, writers are free to express whatever beliefs they may have as their own understanding, provided that the aim in so doing is to further the object of The Open Bible Trust. A copy of the doctrinal basis is available on **www.obt.org.uk** or from:

THE OPEN BIBLE TRUST
Fordland Mount, Upper Basildon
Reading, RG8 8LU, UK.

www.ingramcontent.com/pod-product-compliance
Lightning Source LLC
Chambersburg PA
CBHW060658030426
42337CB00017B/2684